heartstrings

BY FOX HOLLOW

Heartstrings copyright 2023 by Fox Hollow. All rights reserved. No part of this book may be used or reproduced in any manner whatsoever without written permission except in the case of reprints in the context of reviews.
www.foxhollowauthor.com

@foxhollowwrites

Print ISBN: 978-0-983398394
Digital ISBN: 978-0-983398370

Layout: www.formatting4U.com
Editing: Vox Et Liber Publishing
Cover Art: Cassie Hart
Illustrations: Homo.Design

Dictionary Definitions: Oxford Languages

si·no·a·tri·al

adjective ANATOMY

1. adjective: sino-atrial; adjective: sinoatrial

relating to the sinoatrial node, a small body of muscle fibers in the heart responsible for initiating the heartbeat.

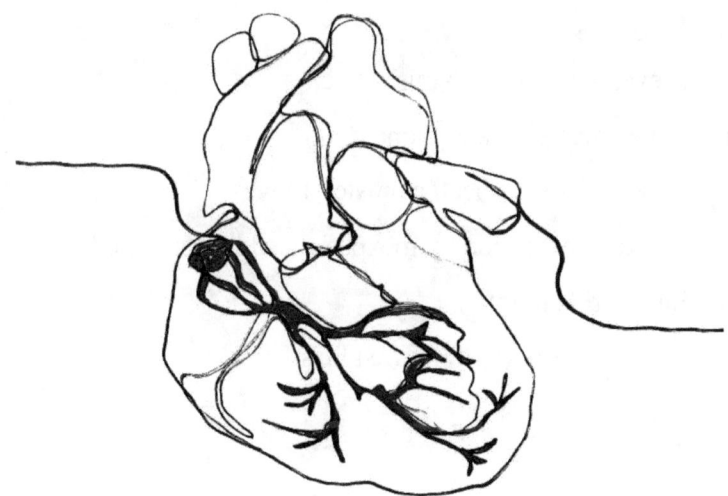

Fox Hollow

Saxophone

I did not wear a dress
To my very first school dance.
    I wore jeans
and a long sleeve shirt that was rescued from Limited Too.
Shaky hands were the perfect accessory
    For a girl on her first date
You put your hands on my hips like a gentleman
And left room for the
    Holy Ghost.
As the evening ended at your house,
you played me your saxophone.
    Jazz has always been a music of love
your off-key notes spun by inexperienced hands turned
a humid Florida night
    into the memory of my first kiss.

Brother

I have never been so scared
To hold something in my life
As I was the day you were born
If I had known what I believed was
Fragile as crystal
Would grow as diamonds
I would have made sure that your life was filled
With more blankets
And softness
    For you to be wrapped in

Blue Eyes

You asked me why

And my response was because you have

    charisma.

And the *bluest eyes* that I have ever seen.

    A shade of blue that caresses the afternoon skies

    when the sun beams and bounces from

    the silver lined clouds

creating a reflection that makes the anxiety

go away.

Heartstrings

Hand drawn

When my head would rest on a
pillow of
hair on your chest
my heart would swell so much
that it filled up every empty space inside
the hollowness of me
I did not know what to do with all of it
instead of packaging its spillage in a
Bright Red Bow

and placing a fragrant rose beneath its ribbon
so that you would not miss it on your chest
My fingers willed to move
by the lust pouring out of the caverns
and
I chose to draw a heart on your skin as you slept

Hey you

Do you have any idea the turns in my stomach and the infatuation that shakes
    my core
        at the thought of you?
Do you understand the feeling of walking on stars?
    Because I do

My pulse is in my throat and I know
This game.
I've played it before on both ends.
Victorious.
Failure.

To have a world shattered by a gaze.

I almost forgot the feeling exists until
my tongue hangs heavy with the sweetness of honey and
every shake
jab
push
pull
clench
release

beat of my heart drumming inside of my chest
keeping time as I count down the minutes until I can see you again

I crave more

Words

You are
To this day
The only boy who ever wrote me a poem.
I keep it in a cigar box
though I do not smoke
Your words lay in a bed of stale smoke, leather, and wood
they sleep with many other memories that I cannot rectify
forgetting quite yet.
Your words that once moved me to tears have moved with me
to five houses
three states
two heartbreaks
And though you handed me presents constantly showing me that you
    Acknowledged
My love for words,
when it came to understanding the
word commitment
You forgot how to read.

Fox Hollow

Little Drummer Boy

thank you for showing
a naïve romantic girl
casual is fine

Heartstrings

Smiting god in a minute

The first time I kissed a girl
It took me a full minute before I thought I was
    Going to hell
Because in sixty seconds
I got lost in the softness of her skin
and how good her hands felt on my face

At thirty seconds
I thought I never wanted to kiss anyone else
At forty-five seconds
I forgot how to breathe
and when that minute hit,
my breath returned and I realized what I had done. I thought
    the joke was on god because
if there was a heaven
the clouds were the curve of her hips and it smelled like
    Chanel Chance.

Inside

It was impossible to get close enough to you
I wanted to exist inside of your skin
Your arms will get tired and move
And when they do
I won't be ready to leave

Companion

In the idle moments
That I dance between
The hands on a clock
I do not fill the time with silence
My busied hands reach
For you

Through the numbers on a screen
in my excitement
Happiness
Anger
Frustration
Creative Spark

It's your ears that I empty the fountain
Of my mind into
Love has many names
And in a sea of letters
I write ours a thousand times-
Friend

Pooch

There is no greater honor
than to have watched you grow
to have your wide eyes
swallow the world around you
and form ideals of your own
And when I watched dad
see you for the first time in your wedding gown
I wept
my heart swelled
because as your older sister I knew
this world belonged to you
and you were hungry for it

Heartstrings

The world in fifteen hours

You met me in the dark at a bar
That I had traded in our world of sunshine for.

The cold of the north had hardened my skin and stripped me of my warmth.

But in you walked with your yellow hair
and southern smile
You wanted to change the world.

You had fifteen hours before you left for the far east
    And I had twelve dollars in my bank account
    But for you,
    I would melt the clock and present you with
    A cup of magic that would send you to another country
    with a kiss from a friend.

My shift ended and we hurried arm in arm down Ditmars at four in the morning and recruited an acquaintance
    for the mayhem we would unleash on New York that
    night.

Fox Hollow

The three of us hopped on a train and held our breath for luck as we went underground

    and entered

    the greatest city in the world

Your blue eyes widened as we climbed the stairs into a barren Times Square.
A perfectly clear stage for the three of us to perform.

We danced and laughed and threw our cares of the world to the skyline
as an offering for her blessing of mischief for this day.

We found our way to the Plaza Hotel and splayed out on the lush cream brocade couches and pretended we were as rich as we felt.

As the sun greeted the clouds softly in the morning sky, we found the entrance of Central Park and wandered through its paths.

  You prayed to angels

    I prayed to Alice and her looking glass.

Heartstrings

We stumbled and smiled and ran into soldiers in three-piece suits of armor who wielded their briefcases like swords as they headed to work.

I'm not sure how we ended up on the steps of the Met,

but with seventy-five cents in my pocket, I paid our entrance and of all the beautiful exhibits I had come to know passed our view

    None of them compared to the joy etched on your face.

Your flight was an hour after we left.

We held a cup of magic in our hands that we shared for a few more seconds before you opened a yellow door to a cab
And drove away.

I never talked to you again.

Fox Hollow

Free Tickets to Tonight's Show

We ate mushrooms in Central Park
And found a hill to sit on to watch our problems melt away
As the world began to distort into something we could
    Finally fit ourselves within
New York showed its magic to us and there had never been
    two luckier people
Because when the caller for the summer performance of
All's Well that End's Well
    Stood at the bottom of our hill
We received two paper keys to the kingdom for free.
We took our seats and gazed forward and
Our world melted
    On the stage
        smoke
    rolled over the pond and ate the actors
        And all the problems we had before in
    one
        gluttonous
            bite.

The Hillsboro Pier

I gave my virginity to a fisherman
His hands were calloused from knotting hooks on wire lines

    But when he caught me in my youth
He was gentle and kind
    and despite being reeled in

    He unhooked me, and put me back in the sea

Clean

I will be soap and a sponge
I will make sure that the counters are so clean that they reflect
    the smiles on our faces as we stare into them
Our home will be banished of any blemishes
So that you may see the world through my eyes
A world that glistens so intensely that it's

    Blinding

And it only gleams more brightly when you walk in a room.

Michigan

Lie to me
and say I'll be your
eternity
And I'll dine on your words
Mouthfuls at a time

Rescue

You didn't cry when I brought you home

But I have cried a million times since.

A monster

decided that your ears should be cut.

I wonder if they ever felt how soft they are.

And when my world has felt as though it was in tatters

when I lay on the bathroom floor with tears summoned by

    the unjustness of the world

You would lay your head on my chest

A monster

    They call you.

Will hurt a child.

    Reactive.

        Not safe.

In a world full of monsters who hurtle words that they do not know the meaning to

You are the only constant stream of joy

Because when I step into a room after laying down from fighting all day

        You will always greet me with a smile

            and an excited tail.

Heartstrings

Bandit

Pull the air from my lungs
and they'll say you left me
breathless
but I'll remember your
thieving
words
and stolen kisses
and report them
remarkable

Heartstrings

hy·per·ten·sion
noun MEDICINE

1.   abnormally high blood pressure.

o a state of great psychological stress.

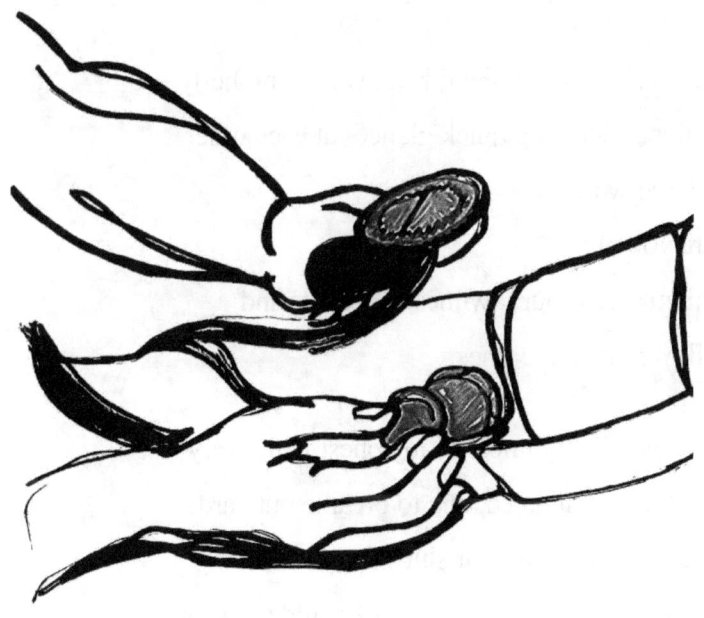

Boxes

There's something to be said about the raw cold
of a winter evening inside of a living room
where few words are barely tempting to warm the air.

We sit in a box, a hollow box that's filled with
doubt, solemn glances and yet, so much love.

The world has shut the lid and we sit somberly
in silence, stealing quick glances at each other
with the words
'Are you okay?'
written across our jawlines in indents and
hollowed in smile lines.

I can feel the tightness of my chest with every
breath that is inhaled, and to breathe outwards
is agony. I stare at your shirt; the pattern is
boxes. Pink boxes that I swear I could see every
piece of me in.
You wear me on your sleeves as you walk out of
my apartment. You leave nothing of me here when you go.

Heartstrings

I am hollow, an empty box, waiting for you to unpackage me with your words. I dance to the rhythm of your heartbeat and the memory of your laugh is the crackle of a fire that keeps me warm when you're in someone else's bed.

And it hurts.

It hurts in the way that a thousand cuts of understanding hurts. For I knew exactly the box I would be packaged in. This box came with a

loose-leaf instruction manual in a language I did not know, but my stubbornness and want was convinced I could learn it.

There is a lot of room in this box. Room for many people, and yet, I've never felt so alone.

I find myself from time to time standing on my tiptoes reaching for the lid. If only I could peak through and catch a glimpse of sunlight, perhaps the cardboard walls of this room wouldn't be so suffocating. Perhaps with some fresh air, the feelings of longing that suck the air from my lungs when I know you're with

Fox Hollow

someone else would vanish, and I could
breathe outside of this box.

I am neatly packed with patience.

I am tied with a bow of understanding.

I am swaddled in a blanket of love and carefully
laid so that I will not break when I am carried on
your wings from place to place.

But there is no window in this box for me
to see the sun rise and set, knowing that
tomorrow is promised.

And the fear that sits in this box with me is
palpable. It is the sheer coat of paint I stare
at searching for chips.

I find no solace here, for I am lost in thought of

how to sit in a box made for many, when I know

a smaller box would be perfect for me

Heartstrings

My Body

I met your mother

    And I know that she never taught you

to tell a teenage girl that she needed to run more to lose weight
Today I look in my mirror
and worship every line
and curve on my body
that you may have gotten to hold
But never got to know

Fox Hollow

The Smell of a Misconstrued Evening

The drenching humidity of exaggeration lingers
Through these buildings created at the
cornerstone with doubt.
It blows its whipping conscience's wind
Through the alleyways of quivering limbs.
Warm the breath of its story
As it lay menacing on the back of your neck.
A sweat break
You inhale its venomous fumes
Through the uncertain nostrils
On your panic ridden face.
A storm of devastation it brings
Through the lights now dimmed with calamities'
Hard
Angry
Scared
Face.

Heartstrings

Bold you stand in the middle of fate's street.
Held to cement floors by the souls of your Bravery.
You wait patiently with good fates
Slighted curl
Written on your lips.
This natural disaster will
Blow your wavering arms
About your body.
You're ready.

Faithless

The morning that my father
Walked into my room
With panic in his eye and a newspaper in his hand
I knew my bedroom ceiling was now made of glass

Like the tension in his footsteps as he passed the threshold.

I held my breath as the hardened voice that I've
known my whole life
    spilled as silk from his mouth to tell me
that you had been in an accident.
As the words were spoken their birth into this world
they created a vacuum that vacated
every molecule of air from the room
    And I could not breathe.

I used what was buried inside my chest to scream
the ceiling above gave way and
    Shattered
Leaving wreckage at my scene.

At fourteen I didn't know what any of this meant.
A car going seventy-five in a fifty
A young boy on a bike in its path
A contorted body that was airlifted to the next town over

Plastic tubes that would serve as your lungs for the next two months.

Heartstrings

"You never forget your first love" they say.

"You've never had to watch your first
love almost die" I say back

Thank God for modern medicine. How can
he not believe in god after he lived? God's
hands were moving with those doctors.

You never had faith.

But when I heard for days straight that it's
    Touch and go
    We just don't know
    Today is not a good day

I felt years of scripture slip away
And I cursed the name of whatever would choose
A boy riding his bike home was on the docket to lose.

At fourteen,
you lived.
We lost each other.
I lost my faith

Fox Hollow

Alcohol

The moment I realized
that you liked Bud Light more than me
I knew that we couldn't be together.
It was Halloween
and you drank so much
    You forgot your name
You could have passed it off that you were dressed as someone else
Or that you didn't need to know your name on a night like this
    But you knew
    That I knew
                     That you were sick.

I had always wanted to move to New York.
I had always said that you were going to be a momentary distraction.
But as you stood on my parents' front steps
And I told you we were done
The glisten in your eye that was once bright when I walked into a room
    Turned into a tear
                     And my heart broke.
Not for what we could have been
But for all the things you would lose
Until you realized the weight of a bottle in one hand
                  Didn't balance the scales
          of the weight of the world in the other.

Liar

You aren't unique.

You learned how to lie from the footprints

That are soaked into the earth from the men

That walked before you.

The momentary hurt that stung my skin

Like the whipping wind of a February night

Faded quickly

And like the wind

You were gone

I don't think about you anymore.

Fox Hollow

Threesome

You invited her into our bed because
She knew where you could get high
My mouth found its way up her thighs
Because her ears had eight piercings
And listened more empathetically than yours

Mood Swings

I've got twenty-five dollars in my bank account and a zero percent chance of success.

I've got longing in my heart and a mind that's a complete mess.

I wish that I had the answers to the rhetorical questions that run through me

I wish I had an understanding of concepts that the world throws at me

What makes the interior of this biological clock tick and why is mine spun with broken gears and hands that can't seem to stay on time?

What is it that I constantly look for and never find?

I wish I had the tools to cope with my afflictions,

I want to drown all the things that I gravitate towards because of my addictions.

Consider me a doctor, a connoisseur of self- medication and throwing myself into situations that make me

> *Feel.*

Fox Hollow

I can't sit in one place for too long, I lose my soul in the grains of sand that fall through the hourglass

And it doesn't matter how much time has passed

I breathe out the words slowly and they pierce my lips as they exit my mouth

> *"I am a harm to myself and others"*

I don't know the difference between what is healthy for me or for what makes me feel healthy,

I don't have boundaries that are drawn in lines of sand by society and books that are designated to help yourself.

I don't have the courage to accept what's wrong with me

I know that balanced medication will turn me into a

Ghost.

So where does this leave me?

Where is this limbo located that causes me to dive head first from cloud nine to hell on a daily basis?

Where is the broom located where I can pick up the pieces of myself after I crash into the floor, head first because nothing that I do can be done at half-mast?

Passion… that girl has passion

Does passion equate to the affiliation with self- deprecation as my lips wrap around a bottle that smells like rocket fuel?

Does passion fly through my fingertips as they constantly reach towards the next best thing that is my flavor of the week?

When it comes to my happiness I gasp and choke on the thought of stability and then become consumed with the thought of it.

Like a weighted scale or loaded dice I throw this game that I consider my life and I

Don't breathe.

I don't know what a calculated council of inhalation means or why it is supposed to make me feel better. I never understand why having to play by the rules is conducive to living

And I don't regret the things I'm buried in as I'm digging.

And I don't see a way out of this prison. So, I sit.

Cool, calm, and collected

Fox Hollow

Making sweet passionate love to my afflictions

And holding so tightly to my inhibitions

waiting for them to fly.

Drunk

You taught me how to ride a bike

Now most days

You can't operate a moving vehicle

After 5 P.M

Secret

My speakers would jolt me
every night
when you summoned my
entire attention with your
>Words
>>Songs
>>>Shows

My playlists today are still filled with cadences that you infused into my soul when I was a teen
For fifteen years you would tell her you were
>going to sleep because you had to brave the Boston cold in the morning for class
>>or had to walk to midtown at the crack of dawn for a deadline

But your fingers would lazily lie to her in one go and stroke my ego with the next And
to this day as she holds your child in her arms
>She doesn't know.
>>I never loved you.

But it was like a bomb to the chest when I heard you two were getting married.
>And despite over a decade of friendship

I would never be allowed at your wedding.

Wasted Night

I elected
to stay the night.
You neglected to tell me
that you bite
back
against
women
with
opinions
I wonder what else I could
have done that
     wasted evening
        instead of you.

Fox Hollow

Golf Carts

              I should have known
That we were made only for teenage summer
Because when we met again ten years later
        In the dead of winter at Grand Central
You had forgotten what I tasted like
And you weren't the same

Heartstrings

car·di·ac ar·rest
noun

2.   a sudden, sometimes temporary, cessation of function of the heart.

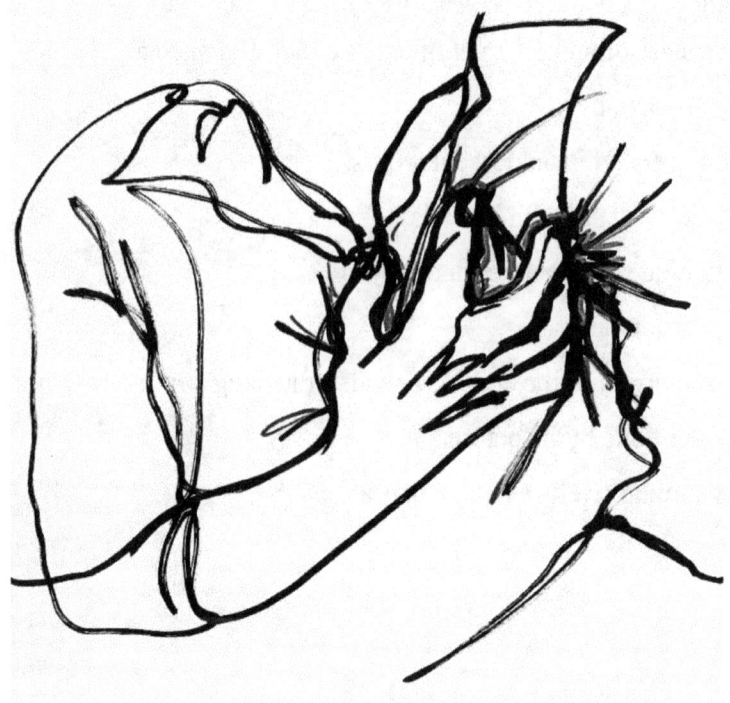

Fox Hollow

You

You live so deeply in my head without paying a cent
with every trickling moment you exist there
You chip away at every bit of *sanity* I have left.
The ghost of what you were to me haunts the halls of this
Broken-down house of my mind
This shambling construct of a home that was once a
    mansion
Of hopes and incandescent words.
    I stand alone in its halls
Listening to the echoes and they are
    Boundless
I am married to the endless sounds of its laughter and merriment
I am undone by its nature
My tongue swells as I try to speak

                                 "End"

Thanks for listening

I had just found out
That there was a life growing inside of me
I was 21 and my invincibility had just died
And had begun to rise as something new in my womb.
I booked an appointment for next week.
That night I planned to pick up a shovel to bury my religion
and decided I'd like to forget.
Of all the poison on the shelf
You were the one I chose to wrap my lips around for the evening.
I don't remember your name
But I do remember
That when I asked you to not finish inside me
You did anyway.

A Statistic

Ninety-three thousand people a year die from overdoses.

You are now a statistic.

You are a number that lays etched on a piece of paper

in the office of a man

compiling data to combat the atrocities that people way bigger than us put into play.

Your life, in all of its wonder

your laugh, infectious,

so much that it kissed everyone's faces as soon as it left your lips

is one upon a sea of many lives that is counted for headlines and placed on the CDC's website under

    "Opioid Epidemic".

Your name, gifted to you by your parents the day you were born is not going to be paraded with the others, you will be a tally on the grand stage of necessity to bring a case against the war on drugs.

        You were such a light.

You were so broken but willed yourself to get up each day.

        You hurt in insurmountable ways.

When the sky came falling down on you it wasn't just the sky that left an impact on your world, but your silhouette that left an impact on ours.

And I am furious.

I am damned to see you become another statistic.

You were too big to fit into such a small number

and I want to hear your voice one more time.

Heartstrings

You left a wreckage behind.

Bent and broken hearts.

Some are angry,

some have accepted.

You were sick.

You were looking for an escape.

I wish you had taken me up on my offer for you to visit.

We'll never know if the northern air would have cleared your head.

Instead,

        you're just another statistic, who lost their battle and is now dead.

No

They say that within 7 years
your body has grown
so many cells that you're made
entirely new.

By this thought I would have a body that
you have never touched.

Science debates if this is true or not, but it was never my body
that *remembered you.*
It was always the images burnt into my brain.

The part of my mind that is slowly nursing me back to health
has locked the worse of you away inside pockets of
blank space
and
decay
that no matter how much I will them to come forward they
stay

> *Hidden.*

For my benefit I don't have to relive the horrors that your
addictions put me through when I was young and didn't have a
full understanding of the word

> *"No".*

I hadn't learned the definition of a boundary

Heartstrings

I hated myself so much that I felt as though you were the only
end road for me because
I didn't deserve anything else.

I think of you now and realize people can change and grow
but when you come across my feeds
I wonder
if your wife knows that you have a history of
punching women in the mouth when you don't like the
words that are coming from it.

I wonder if your daughter will grow up and ever see you under a
sink fixing a broken pipe not knowing that a pipe was your
captor as you brought it to your lips for years and every time
you did you wouldn't come home for 2 days.

The worst is locked away.
I can't summon it like I used to.
I can't wash over the scenes and take them apart trying to figure
out what I did to make you think I would be a great victim.
I wear scars from you on my arm. Fourteen years and seven
stitches later.
A door slamming on my forearm because you didn't want me to
go.

I called your mother that day to tell her you hurt me again.
She was more worried about me calling the police than how I
was because she didn't want your probation violated.

I was too young to know the meaning of
      "*No.*

Fox Hollow

I was never taught how to leave.

> It would take me another decade to learn. It didn't start with you.

It didn't end with you.

Many people have touched and hurt my body since then.

In the world of my hurt and healing you're nothing more than an anecdote that I have and will continue to preach to women
"This is how you know when to run"
"This is too much"
"This is not okay"
"This is how you say *No*"

Fallen heroes

When I was younger
I would look at you and think
I want to be just like her one day
You had the clothes I wanted
A tattoo on your ankle And you loved to read
I could pick up a brush made of dreams and paint on the canvas of my life
exactly how to be you if I applied myself.

Today as I sit on the other end of a phone call
Separated by thousands of miles and a decade of
disenchantment I haven't spoken a word in over 40 minutes
Because your life is more important
Than the words "how have you been"

Fox Hollow

Suffocate

All the words
I would have had for you
Lived and died imprisoned in our living room
I don't even think about you now
My final words
A nail driven into the years we spent together
Intended to bury us so far beneath the earth
That the memory of us would never be able to breathe again
"You're not my problem anymore."
And with that period
Suffocation
and finally, Freedom.

Broken

You gave me
An open heart and your trust
And I thanked you with
A library that I had been chewing on for years
Countless books
Spilling over with lies

Cornerstone

You take for granted
when you hear someone sing often
You get used to their cadence
When their notes fill the empty space in every
corner of a room that is filled with people.
You don't realize that the absence of their song
And the presence of their requiem
Makes the crowded space
Silent
Despite the roaring laughter from those that never met
    you

Green Inferno

I'll always regret that I never got to kiss you

Know that when they found your lifeless body

        on the floor

And they went through your phone

That the pictures of my body that I sent you after midnight

        were assigned to a high

That we did not have

Gaslight

In a room of lies
That you try to lock me in
I will still choose me

Heartstrings

The Christmas Collection

Grief is a caged animal
and the prong that slips
between cage bars
to entice the beast to bellow
changes shapes
                Frequently
it can look like a figurine at a Hallmark during their
        Christmas Collection
            or
It is the echo of a stranger's laugh that bounces
Around walls leaving you searching a room for something you know
              you won't find
Grief looks like
Adidas superstars in black and white
It smells like the crispy seasoning of a combination
        KFC and Taco Bell at 1AM
It is the feeling of being trapped inside
The cage with nowhere to run for days on end
So you lay at its feet and let it feast
        On the flailing memories you have
                left.

re·sus·ci·ta·tion
noun

3. the action or process of reviving someone from unconsciousness or apparent death. "Paramedics were called and aggressive resuscitation was performed"

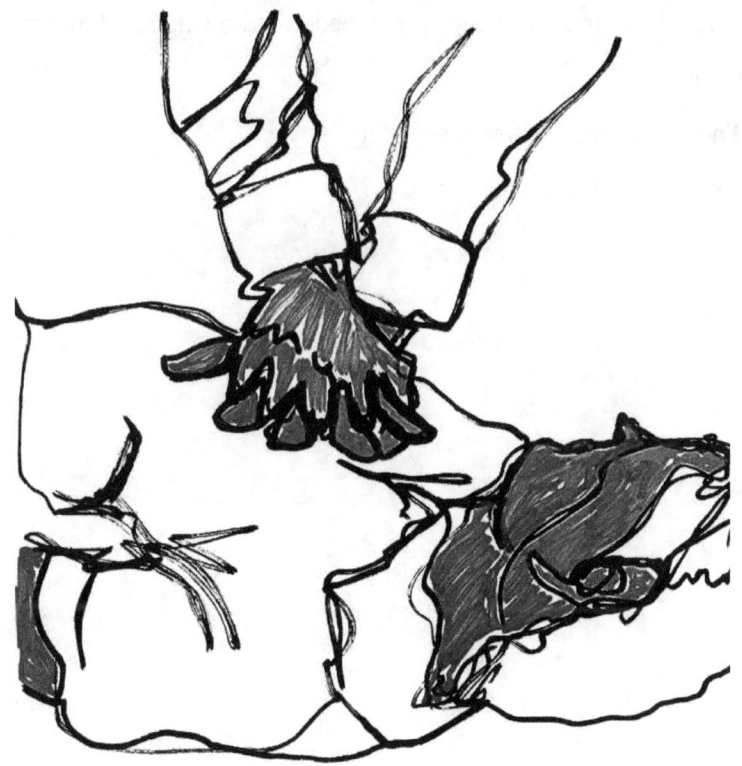

Safety

Loving you is

Breathing for the first time

After years of my head being under water

My impatient hands begged for the surface

Unaware that you would lay in the break of the waves

And when I gasped in the air of freedom with water still in my lungs

The first breath I drew was safety

And it tasted like you.

I Don't Blame You

I don't blame you because
when you walked the isles of a Barnes and Nobles in the 80's
and your fingers landed on book spines about how to raise
children
The words that your eyes would eat were printed with ink that
held hundreds of years of bad practices.
I don't blame you,
for your outburst of frustration when my 'obstinance' became
too much for you to take
so instead of finding words in a kinder voice
your words instead turned to vinegar and ash in your mouth
The aftermath of the explosion they blew at me seconds before.
I don't blame you,
for not having a roadmap of how to keep a child's door on a frame
or having control of their wardrobe because it's what your
mother did to you and her mother did to her.
You did not know how to heal generations of bad behavior with
a few pages of a book.
And when I was 14 and you looked at me and screamed with
every fiber of your being
"I hope that you have a daughter like you one day"
I know you meant it to hurt me, but I took it as the greatest

compliment of my life.

I don't blame you for your ignorance.

But, if I do have a daughter one day, I hope she turns out exactly like me.

I hope she is like what you could have been,
and what your mother could have been if they had their doors left on their frames so that they could think in solitude and have moments of reprieve from the loudness of this world.

For in these moments of quiet the most profound thoughts that shape the directions of life tend to visit.

These feelings of comfort and peace will remain the most important reference point for her throughout the rest of her life as she fights on the battlefield of upheaval in a world designed to pin her down with one foot firmly on her chest.

I hope she looks back to small comforts and remembers what it was like to feel safe so she knows when something is wrong and the alarm bells deafen her ears telling her that whatever is happening in that moment is not what she knows and she needs to leave.

I hope she feels safe enough to voice her thoughts and ideas and be opinionated and never question the meaning of the word *"No"*

or silently resign to a decision because

"that's just the way it is".

I hope she questions everything

and I hope she has a curious mind that isn't stifled a day in her life by my selfish wants or needs.

I have the ability to take generations of hurt that you might not have even realized were wrong, and change them.

I don't blame you,

but I won't let it continue.

Fox Hollow

Chrysalis

Exhale

I stare blankly at the light that creeps from the box in my hand
A box that holds a million words and bounces them from state to state
A box that holds my words as I state a boundary that you gallop at full speed
    Right Over.

I have known you most of my life.
We both have worn many faces.
I have stared at some of your faces with the kind of love that rattles your chest when you inhale. The kind of love that you vow promises upon. The kind of dumb and stupid naivety that breeds phrases like "that person is a once in a lifetime kind of person".

I have stared at other faces with disgust. The faces that exist in the spaces where you should have been standing when you said that you would be there and never showed.
    Your faces that are married to the shadows.
    You are dependable only in your disappearances.

Heartstrings

And as the clock of my life has ticked each exit has been less painful.

    I have grown.

I have learned that the cocoon I have built around myself is not a prison for punishment, but instead a metamorphosis of protection to not allow people like *you* to witness the birth of what happens on the other side.

I am radiant in my growth. I am untouchable by you. I am a chrysalis that you never bothered to have patience for.

    My wings are not for you.

Today I have crawled out of darkness of our past and been born into something new and when I begin to fly, this time

    I will leave you on the ground

Fox Hollow

I'm Sorry

You were a casualty

In my crash course in polyamory

As I shifted my gears and

Sped away from more

I left you at the scene

Failed

You didn't do anything wrong
    I was sick
And didn't know how to reach
    into my throat
To pull out the words
    "I need help"
If I am a villain in your story
    I will happily wear that crown
We never really understood each other
    Even
        when
            we
                were
                    buried
                        beneath
                            the
                                ground.

Fox Hollow

Our Garden

I was born into a world where I was taught
That a woman beside me was competition
The clothes that I wore needed to outshine
 I would hold all the light of a constellation
But my stars would gleam alone
I felt the ghost of friendship in the spaces between my fingers
Though I did not have a name for what was missing
    I grew
And I fell
Into arms that used me for my body and love
    Conditionally
I did not plant seeds in my poisoned soil
For though I did not know it, they would not have grown anyway.
    But I did
And as I did the nutrients of understanding came
The necessity of community and a trust that had to be learned
Today my garden is filled with flowers
                            Beautiful, all of them
I shower them with love and honesty and they do the same for me
                                  And we grow

Love Story

I thought we were the greatest love
story ever composed
Until I realized
My hands were stained with ink and
I loved my story more

Fox Hollow

The closest thing to angels

I have fallen an immeasurable amount
    Due to my lies and deceit
I spent my time in freefall
Paying retribution to the air behind me
    And making promises for second chances
    that I did not deserve
When I hit the ground and found it to be a bed of clouds
Filled with the closest things to angels that actually exist
I questioned what I had done to deserve them
    And they told me it was because I was

me

31

It took thirty-one years
For me decide that I was worth putting on the table
I count myself as chips
Push all of me forward on green felt and speak
"I'm all in"
And when I did
I became richer than any stroke of luck on the strip
I will never gamble with my life again,
But I will bet on myself.

Noodle House

Sitting at lunch alone

I wonder if we'll grow wrinkles

And smiles

Like the elderly couple next to me.

I wonder if you'll love me in the

way Youth promises us

When we're impressionable and

Dream of tomorrow.

I wonder if you'll love the way I bitch

About your socks on the floor

For thirty years.

When I think about quaking hands lifting

A set of chopsticks

And crosswords about

The neighbor's dog

I see our faces sitting next to me

And take a

    Hopeful

                Bite

About the author and book

Fox is a Florida transplant living in New England and has been a lifelong artist. She has written everything from games journalism, fantasy rulebooks, to poetry. *Heartstrings* is a deeply personal book about relationships that have fundamentally altered her brain chemistry and there are poems in it that she had written 14 years ago. This is her debut book. Fox is an avid advocate for mental health awareness, addiction resources, and animal rescue and volunteers in these spheres frequently. When she's not writing she is playing the piano or dressing up her two rescue kittens and Pitbull in ridiculous collars and sweaters.

Acknowledgments

Thank you endlessly to my partner.
Thank you for giving me grace, room to be up all night, and for walking the dog when I was deep in thought. My happiness exists in large part due to the garden that you sow for us and I am incredibly grateful for all that you are.

Thank you to my sister for listening to me scream excitedly about this project even though she couldn't care less. Your voice on the other end of thousands of miles is enough.

Bastion- I love you. You are a foundation to a home for a family that I grew from nothing and I am endlessly grateful for your support, love, compassion, and everything that you are. My life continues to be more thrilling and fuller of love because of you.

Jake and David- Thank you for always picking up your phone and listening to me. I wouldn't have been able to do it without your support.

Mom and Dad- Thank you for gifting me with the arts my whole life and supporting me to live a crazy nomad artist lifestyle. We can finally say I'm published and it wouldn't be possible if you two hadn't thrown up your hands and let me be who I am. Thank you. I love you.

V- You're an asshole. But you're my asshole and my life wouldn't be the same without you. Thank you for always reading my shit.

Avalon North and Sunrise Café- Thank you for the late nights and early mornings of tea and coffee that got me through.

Wade- I love you. I miss you. There will be a Wade-shaped hole in my heart for the rest of my life, and I will write about you forever because of the imprint you left.

Fayth, Chris, Liz, and Cassie- Thank you for helping me during this first-time process. I swear I'll be better at it next time.

www.ingramcontent.com/pod-product-compliance
Lightning Source LLC
Chambersburg PA
CBHW062243300426
44110CB00034B/1843